# BE A BETTER
# TEACHING ASSISTANT

## Alessandra Iantaffi
## Ann Johnston, Emma Baker

**Other titles in this series**

Be a better foundation stage/nursery teacher

Be a better nursery nurse

Be a better form tutor

Be a better secondary classroom teacher

Be a better foundation stage coordinator

Be a better literacy coordinator

Be a better gifted and talented coordinator

# BE A BETTER
# TEACHING ASSISTANT

## Alessandra Iantaffi,
## Ann Johnston, Emma Baker

A division of MA Education Ltd

Teach Books Division, MA Education Ltd, St Jude's Church, Dulwich Road, London SE24 0PB

British Library Cataloguing-in-Publication Data
A catalogue record is available for this book

© MA Education Limited 2006
ISBN 1 85642 328 X

Printed in Malta by Gutenberg Press, Gudja Road, Tarxien PLA19, Malta

# CONTENTS

# ACKNOWLEDGMENTS

The authors would like to thank the Eastern Leadership Centre for giving them the opportunity to teach such interesting and inspiring teaching assistants (TAs) as part of their training towards achieving higher level teaching assistant (HLTA) status. We have learnt much from them as well as all the other TAs that we have encountered in our professional and personal journeys.

Alessandra would like to say a heartfelt thank you to all the TAs who have crossed her path at the University of Hertfordshire and the HLTA candidates from Harrow, Waltham Abbey and Welwyn Garden City, as well as her colleagues who have sustained her passion for education, especially Dr Pam Denicolo and Dr Joy Jarvis. She is forever grateful to Michael and Melissa: without their love, support, patience and understanding, she could not have co-authored this book while juggling work, study and motherhood. Finally, she also thanks her parents, Ettore and Amelia - extraordinary teachers both at home and school, who nurtured within her a love for learning and a fierce passion for teaching.

Ann would like to thank all the wonderful TAs she has worked with in North Yorkshire, Southend and on the HLTA courses.

Emma would like to add her thanks to all the TAs she has worked with in London and Essex, as well as those she has tutored on both the HLTA programme and the Open University Specialist Teacher Assistant Course.

## INTRODUCTION

The role of the teaching assistant (TA) in our schools is currently undergoing a transformation. Over the last 20 years we have seen the move from being 'Primary Helpers' and 'Welfare', to 'Non-teaching', 'Learning Support', 'Curriculum Support' and now 'Teaching Assistants' and 'Higher Level Teaching Assistants (HLTA)'.

The changes in the role have been huge and are continuing in schools across the country, with great variation between them. In most schools, the days of washing paint pots are hopefully long gone and many TAs now take on roles that include group and whole class teaching and sometimes, responsibility for curriculum areas.

This book is intended to be a guide as to how to improve your practice as a TA, whatever your current role may be. Those of you who are new to the role will find it particularly helpful, but there are also tips and useful information for more experienced TAs.

We will look initially at how children learn in 'Looking at learning', especially in relation to the literacy, numeracy and information and communication technology (ICT). What do you need to know to support children in these lessons and how can you find extra information? These are the kinds of issues that we address in a practical, yet theory-based, way.

One of the major issues in schools over recent years has been addressed in the chapter 'Including all pupils'. We live in a diverse society in terms of both culture and ability, and our schools reflect this. You need to be aware of how to adjust your practice to include all pupils whatever your setting and community may be. This section will help you to understand the reasons why inclusion is so important and how to improve what you do to make a difference.

The section on 'Important things to know about schools' will give you guidance on how schools work and will be particularly helpful to those of who are new to the role. Others may find it useful to see the range of practice that exists in schools.

In 'Working with other adults' you will find out more about what roles are in schools these days and how you fit in. It gives you guidance on ways to improve communication with other TAs, teaching staff, management, external specialists, governors and parents and how to work together as a team to benefit the children.

The final two sections give you advice on how to look after yourself and how to move forward. In 'Looking after yourself' we look at the process of appraisal, what trade union support is available and feeling part of a professional team.

How to gain knowledge and move forward in your role is looked at in the final section and this gives you some understanding of the more popular training routes that are available, including progression to HLTA status.

To make the best use of the book you need to have access to the internet. Each section has direct links to websites where you can find an enormous amount of information and resources to support your role.

CHAPTER 1

# LOOKING AT LEARNING

## FACTORS AFFECTING LEARNING

Think about a recent time when you have learnt something new. It could be anything – how to insert pictures into a Word document or learn to salsa dance. If you revisited that learning experience, you could identify several factors that affected your learning either in a positive or negative way. Maybe you were nervous because you have always thought that you weren't very good with computers, yet someone showing you the skill step-by-step really helped. Perhaps trying the salsa steps another couple demonstrated and practising them several times was what allowed you to learn. Regardless of the example you may have chosen, learning is a complex process and the outcome (whether we have successfully learnt something or not) depends on several factors like how motivated were we to learn something new in the first place or how loud the place in which we were learning was.

It is clear from these brief examples that the factors affecting learning are intrinsic (within ourselves) or extrinsic (outside of ourselves). Some common intrinsic factors are confidence, levels of self-esteem, age, maturity, physical and cognitive abilities, previous knowledge, motivation and learning style. Extrinsic factors might include a pleasant learning environment, e.g. comfortable temperature and noise level, adequate lighting, resources available, rapport between learner and teacher, length of instruction/task, time of the day and relevance of content or materials. We also know that learning is social so the learners'

relationship with their peers is another key aspect. How learning is organised, that is whether it is individual or how people are paired or grouped, can have a significant impact on this complex process.

One of the mentioned intrinsic factors, learning style, is closely linked to another notion – that of multiple intelligences, a theory conceived by Howard Gardner in *Frames of Mind: the Theory of Multiple Intelligences* (1983). He identified seven different types of intelligences, which people may display: visual, verbal, logical, bodily, musical, interpersonal and intrapersonal.

Both of these notions – multiple intelligences and learning styles – are based on the belief that we do not all learn in the same way or even show intellectual ability in the same way. Therefore, knowing what type of learner you are means that you can use appropriate resources to facilitate your learning process. When working with pupils in school, it can be important to know what type of learners we have in the classroom and to encourage older pupils to own their learning process by being aware of how, and not just what, they learn. This could be done, for example,

by encouraging them to take the quiz either online (*Box 1.1*) or on paper, by facilitating a discussion on positive and negative learning experiences in the past or by asking them to draw a mind map of all the things that help them to learn.

---

### Box 1.1 Learn more

- You can find out more about learning styles and multiple intelligences at:
  http://www.ldpride.net/learningstyles.MI.htm
  and
- http://www.vark-learn.com/
  You can also take your learning style quiz online!

---

Too hot, too cold, too still, too quiet, too thirsty, too hungry and you *won't* be able to learn much!

## ICT AND LEARNING

Information and communication technology, more commonly referred to as ICT, is an ever expanding and fast developing world. It is also a world that has much to offer to learning (*Box 1.2*). Much ICT is new to us, albeit not to our pupils and it may be something that we have not needed to deal with much when we were learners in primary or secondary school. However, all of our pupils were born in a context where ICT is present, in various forms, throughout their lives. This has been recognised by the government through the development of an ICT curriculum as well as the training pack *ICT Across*

## Box 1.2 ICT resources on the net

- http://www.curriculumonline.gov.uk/Subjects/ICT/Subject.htm
  ICT curriculum online for key stages 1 to 4.

- http://www.becta.org.uk/
  British Educational Communications and Technology
  Agency.

- http://www.school-resources.co.uk/
  An educational resource website offering interactive
  information technology quizzes, and a library of learning and
  teaching resources to staff and students.

- http://www.woodlands-junior.kent.sch.uk/teacher/ict.html
  A useful page of ICT links for teachers in primary schools.
  Some of the links are relevant for secondary schools as
  well.

- http://www.teachernet.gov.uk/teachingandlearning/
  subjects/ict/
  Guidance and resources for ICT teachers at all key stages.
  Plenty of links for both primary and secondary schools.

- http://www.blueskiesproject.org.uk/
  A website dedicated to the use of ICT with deaf children and
  young people.

*the Curriculum* (Department for Education and Skills (DfES), 2004a). The role played by ICT in learning has also been acknowledged in the report, *Five Year Strategy for Children and Learners* (DfES, 2004b).

ICT, of course, does not just include personal computers or the Internet. Other technology, such as digital photo and video cameras, audio and video recording equipment and interactive whiteboards, are nowadays part of many classrooms. Nevertheless, you may sometimes feel daunted by the fact that your pupils might know more than you when it comes to technology! We would like to invite you to see this as a priceless opportunity to encourage your pupils' knowledge and skills to be shared with each other, including the teaching staff, in the classroom. ICT lends itself well, in fact, to engaging cross-curricular projects, which can often offer pupils the opportunity to learn both independently and as part of a group while also demonstrating their strengths and abilities. TAs have an invaluable role to play in this regard as they are often asked to support individual pupils and groups engaging with tasks that include the use of ICT, or are responsible for differentiating learning for some pupils in the classroom.

For example, a school has used digital cameras with pupils to create short animation films with plasticine characters created by the pupils themselves. Depending on the age of the pupils, they could also write a script for the short film and a soundtrack. They could then create publicity materials for their film and even share it with other classes and parents. A simpler example of the use of ICT to differentiate tasks in the classroom would be to ask pupils who may find writing difficult to record an audio message or, in the case of deaf pupils whose dominant language is British Sign Language (BSL), to video a message describing what they have seen on a class outing in order to develop skills in expressive language while other peers might write a letter about it.

As well as using ICT to support teaching, it is also important to consider the ethical and social aspects of using technology. Pupils need to develop an understanding, for example, of the emotional impact of electronic and mobile communication through the discussion of issues such as 'netiquette', that is the implied and unwritten rules of appropriate behaviour on the Internet, or how to keep safe from strangers when using instant messaging programmes. Whatever our own relationship with ICT may be, our pupils were born into a digital age and they need to develop the knowledge and skills appropriate to such an age if they are to be fully participating citizens in our society.

# THE 'THREE RS' IN THE 21ST CENTURY

The teaching of reading, writing and arithmetic, often called 'the three Rs', has always formed the basis of education and it is no different today. In order to be successful citizens and achieve well in life, children must be literate and numerate. The only difference now is the approach to learning and teaching of these subjects. As a TA you will probably spend a large amount of time with children who are struggling with these basic skills. In this section you can gain a quick overview of new approaches to learning and be introduced to a range of useful resources.

In England And Wales, basic skills are defined as '*...the ability to read, write and speak in English/Welsh and to use mathematics at a level necessary to function and progress at work and in society in general...*' (www. basic-skills.org.uk) (Basic Skills Agency, 2006).

## Background to new approaches to learning the 3Rs

In 1998, when the political agenda was 'education, education, education!' the *National Literacy Strategy* (NLS) (DfES,1998a) and the *Literacy Hour* (DfES, 1998b) were introduced into primary schools to support teachers in raising standards to meet the challenging targets set by the government. The following year the *National Numeracy Strategy* (NNS) (DfES, 1999) was introduced and provided teachers with detailed guidelines for developing the mathematical skills of children. At the same time, the government implemented a £350 million programme to increase and improve the support offered by TAs to teachers and pupils particularly in literacy and numeracy. The numbers of full time TAs had increased by 20000 by 2002. TAs are considered an important part of the Government's strategy to improve standards.

The work of TAs in supporting these strategies was invaluable and training courses were available for them to give them an understanding of how best to work with children to give them these basic skills. In fact, a number of the special lessons were delivered TAs solely in both literacy and numeracy. (Details of all the NLS and NNS frameworks and TA support programmes can be found in your school or on DfES standards site www. standards.dfes.gov.uk/primary.)

The key stage 3 strategy was launched in 2002 and provides a framework for looking at literacy and numeracy across all subjects in the curriculum. There was a much greater emphasis on the process of learning rather then just what pupils needed to know.

In 2003 *The Primary National Strategy* (DfES, 2003a) was introduced. The curriculum had been dominated for five years by the focus on literacy and numeracy and while standards had risen initially, they had remained static for a couple of years.

The publication *Excellence and Enjoyment – A Strategy for Primary schools* (DfES, 2003b)* sets out a vision for primary education where high standards are obtained through a rich, varied and exciting curriculum, which develops children in a range of ways. It actively encouraged schools to take back ownership of the curriculum and be creative and innovative in how they taught. The NLS and NNS were brought together and given a greater emphasis on how children *learn* the basic skills, rather than how teachers should *teach* them. The strategy extended the support previously given to basic skills to PE, music, ICT, the arts and creativity, and modern foreign languages. All the research was saying that children needed to learn the basic skills as part of an engaging and relevant curriculum.

---

* The aims of the *Primary National Strategy* are explained in the publication *Excellence and Enjoyment* (DfES, 2003b). Ask for a copy at school or download one from www.standards.dfes.gov.uk/primary.

# TALKING TO LEARN

One of the most effective ways of supporting pupils to learn the basic skills is to give them frequent opportunities for talking, explaining, questioning and even laughing (*Box 1.3*)!

---

### Box 1.3

We retain
10% of what we read
20% of what we hear
30% of what we see
50% of what we hear and see
70% of what we say
90% of what we say and do

Source unknown

---

We have looked at the factors that enable us to learn and now we need to be able to transfer these into the classroom. If we want pupils to retain knowledge then we must give them opportunities for talking. It is surprising that all the recent research about learning says that to be successful pupils need to be actively involved, yet a number of classrooms are still silent places. The Literacy Hour potentially provided boundless opportunities for pupils to talk about their work and actively engage in their learning. Instead, in a number of classrooms, talking was actually rare. As a TA you are in a good position working with groups or one to one to enable your pupils to 'talk to learn'.

## Asking questions is key

- What?
- Where?
- Why?
- Which?
- Who?
- How?
- Find?
- Tell me?

These key words are easy to remember and will enhance learning in any literacy or numeracy session. They can be used to ask questions in preparation for a task, during a task and for reflecting back on a task. Having the prompts on laminated cards is helpful and also reinforces the words for the pupils.

When asking the questions, try to make them open-ended so that the pupils have to work harder at thinking about the answers.

For example:

- *'What do you think will happen next?'*
- *'What makes you think that?'*
- *'Which ways could you do this?'*
- *'Tell me how you know that...?'*

Always remember the 'wait time' after asking a question. Count slowly to ten in your head to give the pupil time to think about their answer. TAs working on the Open University Specialist Teaching Assistant Course (STAC) found this one of the most effective strategies for enabling pupils to learn. Previously, they had assumed the pupil did not know the answer and provided it themselves almost immediately. Developing this use of questioning was often evaluated as having the most impact on their practice.

## Give pupils opportunities to use talk to:

- Explain what it is they are going to do.
- Talk about the things they don't understand.
- Ask questions about their work.
- Understand the texts they are reading.
- Speak ahead of writing something down.
- Explain how they have done something.
- Understand what they are able to do and where they have problems (*Box 1.4*).

## Box 1.4 Use talk partners

The next time you ask a question – whether you are working with two children, a small group or a whole class – tell the pupils to talk about the answer with the person next to them. Give them one to two minutes for talking (it will be quite noisy but don't worry; the pupils will be engaged and learning!) and then ask for answers as normal. This strategy ensures that all the pupils engage with the questions and all have to 'work hard' rather than just sit back and switch off. You may need to model how to be a talk partner in the first instance.

If the teachers you work with use this as a strategy you can act as talk partner to the least able pupils to give them confidence and to show them how it is done.

## Box 1.5 Supporting reading and writing

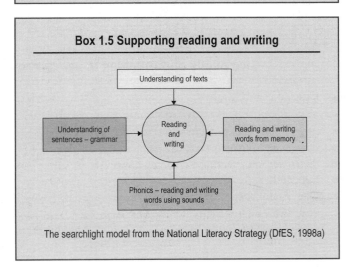

The searchlight model from the National Literacy Strategy (DfES, 1998a)

Central to the NLS is the model of reading and writing represented by the searchlight model (*Box 1.5*). The model demonstrates that in order to read and write you have to coordinate a variety of strategies:

- Fast phonic decoding and spelling.
- Instant recognition and recall of whole words or parts of words.
- Knowledge of sentences or grammar in order to make sense of what is being read or written.
- Understanding of how texts work to help both comprehension and composition.

Pupils need all of these strategies to learn to read and write. The Literacy Hour supports the teaching of these strategies through word level work (phonics and word recognition), sentence level work (grammar; text level work) and introducing pupils to a wide range of fiction and non-fiction. The NLS (DfES, 1998a) sets out what pupils need to know for each school year in each of these three areas.

There is still a great deal of research going on into how children learn to read and new initiatives are always being introduced.

The framework is being revised and the Literacy Hour is less prescriptive now but the principles of the searchlight model remains key to learning.

The NLS has produced numerous resources to help teachers and teaching assistants support learning and you need to speak to the literacy coordinator about what is available in your school.

You should have your own copy of the NLS Framework and another very useful resource is the *NLS Professional Development resource pack 1* (DfES, 2003c), which contains CDs and DVDs to help you understand all aspects of literacy teaching.

The Standards Site (http://www.standards.dfes.gov.uk) is excellent. Follow the links for literacy and you will be able to see the wide range of resources – both for teaching and your own professional development. If, for instance, you are unsure about your knowledge of grammar, there is an interactive online course for you! If you want to know more about the approach to phonics in the early years, there are details of the latest research.

---

### Box 1.6 Useful Resources

- Guided reading videos showing a year 1 group reading *The Go Kart* and a year 5 group reading *The Firework Maker's Daughter* – both of these are on DVD in NLS Professional Development resource pack 1 (DfES, 2003c) – there will be copies in your school.

- *Early Writing and Grammar for Writing* (DfES, 2001) – especially the final section which summarises the organisation and language features of different types of text, e.g. recount; instructions and is a useful reference for TAs supporting pupils

- *The Spelling Bank* (DfES, 1999a) - this contains lists of words and ideas to help the teaching of spelling in key stage 2. It also includes spelling rules and conventions, which are very useful reminders!

- *Supporting Literacy and Numeracy: A guide for learning support assistants* by Glenys Fox and Marian Halliwell (2000) – a really practical guide to enable TAs to work more effectively in supporting basic skills.

Finally, the best way to support learning in reading and writing is to enable pupils to:

- read, read, read
- write, write, write!

Whatever their age, read to children and enthuse them about books; flood them with wonderful texts, build on their interests – there are books on every topic.

Write with children, show them the reasons for writing, make sure they have something to say by getting them to 'talk ahead of writing' and help them to be able to write any word.

## SUPPORTING MATHEMATICS

This is one of the areas that cause the most diverse range of emotions in adults and children alike. What's your immediate thought when the topic of maths comes up? Are you a lover or a hater? If you had to complete this sentence what would you choose?

Maths is...boring/difficult/interesting/fun/a nightmare?

Many of us will have very strong reactions when it comes to maths and we need to be aware of that when working with children. Some of us will have ingrained prejudices about maths because of the way we were taught at school, or because of experiences in later life. Others will love it and relish the challenge it provides. However, there is no escaping it – how many times do you use numbers in your everyday life? For this reason it's vital that maths is made accessible and fun in schools so that future generations can go on to love it, not hate it!

One of the major issues with maths and number work is how we record it. If you asked young children to record their counting they would use a wide range of methods including pictures and diagrams that are personal to them. Numbers and symbols don't come naturally and how to use them needs to be taught. Once they've learnt the symbols for the numbers they then have to go on to learn the symbols for the operations, just to confuse them even more! Martin Hughes is one of the leading researchers in this area, and in several of his projects he has found that when children make mistakes with addition and subtraction problems, it is often as a result of confusion over what the symbols mean – not the maths itself (Hughes, 1986). Tied in with this is the language we use to describe the operations. How many words can you think for adding or subtracting? This use of language can be one of the main issues for children who have difficulties with maths.

The other major issue with maths is the abstract nature of a lot of the work we do in school. Children are usually much better at using maths to solve practical, meaningful everyday problems rather than abstract sums on a piece of paper, even when the mathematical operations used are very similar.

Consider this as an example:

Which of these would you rather answer?

- *1.5 ÷ 0.25*
- *How many 25ps are there in £1.50?*

Many of you will look at number 1 and immediately be put off by the division sign, yet the maths involved in both of them is exactly the same. One cause of the difficulty with problem 1 is that it looks very like school maths. Many people will have learnt that there is a right and wrong way to do maths and if you can't remember the right way you are stuck.

Even when mathematical problems seem to be abou... world they often contain special ways of talking that ... must learn to decode. So, be aware of this and ma... maths as real as you can to get the best out of the children you support.

Recent developments in the ways maths is taught have meant that children's own ideas for ways to solve problems are encouraged and the emphasis has shifted away from rigid teaching of particular methods (*Box 1.7*).

---

### Box 1.7 Encourage children with maths

- Ask them to explain their methods.
- Share different methods with the rest of the group.
- Praise their efforts to develop their own methods.
- Help them to record their ideas on paper, using apparatus or on whiteboards etc.
- Never discourage them from using bricks, their fingers or any other apparatus – it needs to be real and they will stop doing this when they are ready for more abstract thinking.
- Try to show children the link between their methods and more formal ways of solving problems.
- Encourage them to check their own answers by trying out different methods.
- Help them to judge for themselves whether an answer is right rather than waiting for an adult to tell them.

---

# The maths curriculum and the Numeracy Hour

Although many of us think of maths as being 'number work' it is important to remember that there are four main areas identified in the *National Curriculum* (DfES, 1998c) that all carry equal importance:

- using and applying maths
- number
- shape, space and measures
- handling data.

Since the introduction of the *National Numeracy Strategy* (DfES, 1999b) the teaching of maths in primary schools has changed dramatically, and this is now beginning to have knock-on effects at secondary level. There have also been tremendous changes in the way that TAs now support in maths lessons (*Boxes 1.8 and 1.9*).

---

### Box 1.8 Support strategies

There is a wide range of strategies that can be used at different stages of the numeracy lesson:

#### Whole class

- Discreet one-to-one support to help those who have difficulty concentrating.
- Provide apparatus for those who have trouble with abstract concepts.
- Co-present with the class teacher.
- Observe the responses of the children and note any difficulties that need feeding back to the teacher.

---

- Sign, translate or reinforce key vocabulary points that may have been missed.

### Main teaching activity

- Oversee the work of groups while the teacher focuses on one group.
- Re-explain the task and provide differentiated resources as necessary.
- Question children and maintain an appropriate pace.
- Observe and assess progress and give feedback to the children.
- Link the lesson to previous work and help children to prepare for the plenary.

### Plenary

- Co-lead the class with the teacher.
- Help the children to reflect on their learning within the lesson.
- Reinforce key vocabulary and learning points as needed.

---

### Box 1.9 Numeracy resources

- *NNS Teaching Mental Calculation Strategies - guidance for teachers at key stages 1 and 2* (DfES, 2004c).
- *NNS Teaching Written Calculations – guidance for teachers at key stages 1 and 2* (DfES, 1999). These will help you understand the key changes in approaches to teaching both mental and written calculations and understand how pupils make progress with these as they move through school.

cont../.

- *Mathematical Vocabulary* (DfES, 2000a) You should be able to find one in school. If not tel. 0845 6022260 or download on line at www.dfes.standards.gov.uk. The introductory chapter has an excellent section on questioning to develop mathematical understanding with practical examples of questions to extend thinking. There is also a very good explanation of open and closed questions and lists of the correct mathematical vocabulary used by each year, from reception to year 6.

- A very good resource to support you across the primary age range is *Assisting Numeracy: A handbook for teaching assistants* by Ruth Alpin (1998). This is an excellent resource for TAs working in primary schools and covers the whole age range from reception to year 6. It gives the background you need to understand the basics in assisting children then it has games and activities matched to year groups. Of particular interest are the five minute activities and a number of TAs we work with have found these to be invaluable when left with a whole class for the odd five minutes. As well as mathematical games and activities, it has useful tips; questions to ask; things to notice and a very helpful glossary

### On the net

- www.nc.uk.net – this will give you detail and explanation about all areas of the National Curriculum.
- www.standards.dfes.gov.uk/primary/ – follow the links for mathematics. A very useful resource is identifying and supporting children's gaps in mathematical knowledge as well as a number of resources here on all aspects of numeracy, including downloads to muse on interactive whiteboards.

- www.mathsnet.net – MathsNet.net is an independent educational website providing free mathematics resources to the education community. Its aim is to offer truly interactive resources that are both wide and deep in terms of their applicability and usefulness. MathsNet is not an online textbook; it is interactive, requiring the user to participate rather than be a passive observer.

# BRAIN GYM

Pupils, for a variety of reasons, are not always in the optimum state to learn the basic skills. Using Brain Gym exercises at any time can enhance readiness for learning; physical movement increases oxygen in the blood stream and leads to improved concentration.

These exercises are taken from the research undertaken by Edu-Kinesthetics Inc in the US, who concluded that whole brain learning through repatterning and Brain Gym activities enables students to access parts of the brain previously unavailable. These can the lead to a profound change in behaviour and learning.

## Activities

- Cross-crawl or skip-a-cross – coordinate the movement so that when one arm moves, the leg on the opposite side of the body moves at the same time. Move to the front, side and back. Move eyes in all directions. Touch your right knee with your left hand and vice-versa. Touch right knee with left elbow and vice-versa.

- Lazy 8's – draw the figure 8 three times in the air or on paper with each hand about three times, then with both hands together.
- Double doodle – draw with both hands at the same time, in, out, up and down in the air.
- Alphabet – write large letters of the alphabet together in the air.
- Elephant – bend your knees, glue your head to your shoulder and point across the room. Use your ribs to move your whole upper body as you trace a 'lazy 8'. Look past your fingers. Repeat with the other arm.
- Neck rolls – breathe deeply, relax your shoulders and drop your head forward. Allow your head to slowly roll from side to side as you breathe out any tightness. Your chin draws a smooth curve across your chest as your neck relaxes.
- Find more at http://www.salt.cheshire.gov.uk/mfl/ TOOLKIT/BRAINGYM.HTM

# TAS AS REFLEXIVE PRACTITIONERS

Schools are learning environments not just for pupils but for educators as well. TAs, in particular, often do most of their learning in schools. You may already have gone on to a range of courses as a TA, such as the HLTA training or the Specialist Teacher Assistants (STA) certificate, yet we would probably agree that much of what you have learnt has been through practice. This type of learning may take a variety of forms, such as observing teachers or other TAs, trying out an idea with pupils, reading a policy document, carrying out research on the Internet or simply discussing pupils' needs with the Special Educational Needs Coordinator (SENCO) or with parents.

The ability to pause for a moment and look at what works or doesn't and how we might change our practice next time is what makes us reflexive practitioners, that is people who are able to learn from their own practice*. This ability is fundamental in schools as it enables us to cope with a wide range of pupils and needs.

Your school may already support a culture in which reflexive practice can thrive, for example, by encouraging mentoring, joint planning between teachers and TAs or peer observation. If it doesn't though, do not underestimate the power of being able to talk some aspect of your school day through with a classroom teacher or another TA.

We learn best from our own practice when we are also able to discuss it with others in school. This is because we may be able to tap into another perspective on something that we may find challenging or simply because translating our thoughts into words develops our own thinking. For example, you might even consider asking a colleague, such as the SENCO or a classroom

---

* If you would like to learn more about the advantages of taking time to think read *Time to Think* by Nancy Kline (1999) or visit her website at http://www.timetothink.com.

teacher, to mentor you if you want to develop your practice in a particular area, such as developing resources for a particular curriculum subject or group of pupils.

### Handy Hints

- A number of factors affect learning; some of which we can control and some we can't.

- We need to take account of different learning styles and intelligences.

- Information and communication technology (ICT) has transformed opportunities for learning.

- The National Literacy Strategy and National Numeracy Strategy have changed the approach learning basic skills.

- Talking about learning is important.

- The National Literacy Strategy searchlight model underpins the process of learning to read and write.

- It is important to give children confidence in their ability to understand maths; support in numeracy is key to this. Wide ranges of resources are available to teaching assistants to help pupils make progress in the basic skills.

- Brain Gym activities enhance learning.

CHAPTER 2

# INCLUDING ALL PUPILS

## DIVERSE PUPILS, INCLUSIVE CLASSROOMS

Our classrooms look different to what they would have looked like twenty or thirty years ago. Some of these differences are obvious; others more subtle. Our displays might show writing in a variety of languages. Both boys and girls may be found knitting or doing woodwork. Children displaying a range of physical, cognitive and emotional abilities sit around the same tables. Our classrooms reflect our striving towards more inclusive schools. The inclusion agenda, as well as being part of social changes, is also driven by the government's policies such as The Children Act 2004 and the *Special Educational Needs Code of Practice* (DfES, 2002a).

However, what does it mean to develop and nurture an inclusive learning environment and is inclusion different from integration? In order to answer the first part of this question it is useful to address the second part first.

Integration suggests the assimilation of difference into something that already exists. For example, a child with Asperger's syndrome (AS) might be integrated in a mainstream classroom and be encouraged to develop coping mechanisms that will allow him or her to fit in the school. Although this might indeed be an important target for this pupil to achieve, including this pupil would require more than just his or her presence in the classroom. For example, the whole school community, that is teachers, TAs, pupils and parents, need to develop some understanding of AS and the class might be arranged in a particular way to accommodate the child's needs. Stories including positive characters with AS could be added to the school's resources so that the child's difference can be acknowledged and celebrated and his or her self-esteem nurtured.

We can, therefore, begin to see that inclusive learning environments are those in which diversity is acknowledged and celebrated. The message (if we were to put it into an easy slogan) would be 'we are all different but we all have value'. This is not an easy task, especially as we might be dealing with large classrooms of thirty pupils in early years settings, as well as trying to respond to other pressures such as the National Curriculum or specific achievement targets to satisfy demands created by the league tables.

Furthermore, inclusion encourages us to look at our own prejudices; the values and beliefs that we all carry within us and that have been developed over the course of our lives, through our upbringing, schooling and life experiences. We need to understand what we might consider 'normal' if we are to truly have high expectations of all pupils. If we have never met a high achieving person with AS, for instance, it may be difficult to look beyond the difficulties in social interaction and the unusual patterns of behaviour that a pupil with AS might display.

Inclusion calls us to be what John M Hull calls a 'trans-world professional', in his paper 'Teaching as a Trans-World Activity', which was published in the journal *Support for Learning* (Hull, 2004). Being a trans-world professional means being able to use your imagination in order to understand the way your pupils may experience and learn about the world. This understanding is vital to identify effective ways of working with your pupils when supporting their learning and can be encouraged through a variety of activities, such as reading both fictional and non-fictional accounts by and about a range of people talking about their experiences of schools (Hull, 2004).

For example, reading the popular novel *The Curious Incident of the Dog in the Night Time* by Mark Haddon (2003) may have already helped you in appreciating what the world might look like to a young person on the autistic spectrum. Of course, different people with similar disabilities, such as autism, do not necessarily experience the world in the same way. Therefore it is important to approach each pupil with both some knowledge and an open mind, willing to engage in a process of discovery. Such a process of discovery applies to each pupil in your classroom, not just to those with particular abilities or needs. After all, it can be just as difficult to imagine what the world might look like to a 13-year-old boy if, for example, you are a woman in your thirties, or to understand a 7-year-old girl who has been brought up as Pagan or Jewish if you are a Christian or a Muslim. However, as TAs, you may often be asked to support pupils with SEN within a mainstream school. It is to this aspect of your practice that we shall turn our attention in the next section (*Box 2.1*).

---

### Box 2.1 Inclusion resources on the net

- http://www.everychildmatters.gov.uk/
  The official website explaining the implications of *Every Child Matters.* This site is relevant for all TAs, from early years to secondary school practitioners.

- http://www.teachernet.gov.uk/docbank/index.cfm?id=3724
  You can download the SEN Code of Practice from this link or order your free copy from the DfES (http://www.dfes.gov.uk/publications/).

- http://www.bristol-lea.org.uk/services/eit/definitions.html
  A site defining inclusion in relation to schools. Includes some interesting quotations.

> ■ http://inclusion.uwe.ac.uk/csie/indexlaunch.htm
> The Centre for Studies on Inclusive Education has
> developed an Index for Inclusion. This is a set of materials
> to guide schools through a process of inclusive school
> development.

## Understanding special educational needs

An official definition of SEN can be found in the DfES Code of Practice (2002b). This states that '*...children have special educational needs if they have a learning difficulty which calls for special educational provision to be made for them...*'.

Such a definition, as well as the contents of the Code of Practice is influenced by legislation, such as the Education Act 1996 and the Disability Discrimination Act 1995. The Special Educational Needs and Disability Act (SENDA) 2001 is also relevant to defining and working with SEN. Whereas the SENDA establishes the legal right for disabled students not to be discriminated against in education, the Code of Practice offers guidance on good practice both in identifying pupils with SEN and supporting their learning. As a TA, you are likely to be involved at various stages in the pupils' educational lives, such as when a specific need is identified, or supporting the achievement of targets set out in an Individual Education Plan (IEP). It is therefore important to be familiar with some of the key concepts included in the Code of Practice.

The guidance in the Code stems from some fundamental principles – these highlight the right for a pupil with SEN to have their needs met in a mainstream setting, including access to an appropriate, relevant, broad and balanced curriculum, the importance of seeking the pupil's views and taking them into account and the vital role played by parents. The principles are also closely related to the critical success factors detailed in the Code of Practice (DfES, 2002b) such how the school ethos, that is its culture, management and practices, needs to ensure that the needs of all children are met. Other critical factors to success are early identification of any needs, regular reviews and working in partnership with parents. As a TA, you have a role in all of these factors. Often you may be the person who has more opportunities to observe the pupils while working, which can support the early identification of SEN, such as dyslexia or visual impairments. You may also be involved in reviewing the progress of the pupils you support, either with the teacher or other professionals, such as a peripatetic teacher of the deaf or a speech and language therapist. Finally, you may also be the person that parents may feel comfortable talking to at the school gate. As such, another important aspect for you to understand is that, even when a need may be identified, such as difficulties with reading, the purpose is not to have the pupils assessed and statemented as quickly as possible.

The Code recommends a graduated response to SEN. This means that, in the first place, all teachers should differentiate teaching and learning activities in order to meet the diverse needs of pupils in their classrooms.

If a pupil needs more than the teacher can normally provide, such as individual support or specific learning materials, the school should establish what these needs are and provide what is necessary. This step is defined as 'School Action' in the code. If this step is not sufficient, it is followed by the next step, 'School Action Plus', when outside support services, such as specialist teachers or educational psychologists (provided by the education authority) may be involved.

If, after all these steps have been taken, the school can demonstrate that, despite the employment of appropriate programmes and strategies, progress remains unsatisfactory for a particular pupil, a request for a statutory assessment can be made. After the assessment, a 'statement' may be issued. This would detail the pupil's special educational needs and what is necessary to meet them. Any of the steps highlighted above would need regular reviews involving not only teaching staff and, in some cases, specialists, but also parents and the pupils themselves.

If you are dealing with the parents or carers of a child with SEN, it is useful to bear in mind that they may be struggling with the same prejudices that are so prevalent in society about disability. This means that SEN can be an emotional issue to deal with for everyone concerned. Although things have changed over the last 10 years, especially under the influence of the Disability Discrimination Act and the campaigning by disabled activists themselves, there is still some stigma attached to having a disability. Images of wheelchairs, dependency and lack of ability are often prevalent in the media, as well as in people's minds when thinking about disability. Disabled activists have complained, for example, that charitable fundraising initiatives help to promote the image of disabled people needing charity rather than social justice. This is why they have challenged people to reconsider the way that they view disability, not from a medical or individual standpoint but from a social standpoint. Simply put, if someone is in a wheelchair you could see their main problem as being their inability to walk (medical, individual model) or the fact that there are so many stairs around and not enough lifts or wide-enough doors (social model).

When thinking about your classroom, it can be helpful to consider how you talk about your pupils with SEN. Do you refer to their deficits, such as their inability to see clearly if they are visually impaired, or to the obstacles that are present in the classroom (example the lack of books or games in larger print)? You may be surprised about how different something as familiar as your classroom or the route to school may seem if you try to shift your perspective.

## Differentiation

We have already talked about how people learn in a variety of ways in *Chapter 1*. This idea is the basis for differentiation. If we all learn in different ways, one approach to teaching will not suit everyone. Differentiating means taking into consideration your learners and tailoring your teaching and learning activities to them.

This can be achieved in a variety of ways. If your pupils have very different abilities, specific needs or more simply, very different levels of knowledge, you may need to differentiate by objective; that is you might have different learning intentions for them. Even when your learning intention is the same for the whole class, you may still need to differentiate by task. For example, someone may be unable to hold a pair of scissors for a cut and paste activity but is perfectly able to understand ordering pictures in a sequential manner. You may also need to differentiate through the resources used. In the example just used, a pupil who cannot physically cut and paste pictures to order them sequentially may be able to do this activity on a computer instead. You may also want to differentiate by outcome. This means that you may ask some of your pupils to produce a one-page story and others to write a brief paragraph or draw a storyboard in pictures instead.

Differentiation is also useful to bear in mind when talking about a topic or demonstrating an activity as it can help with varying the pace and interest of the lesson. For example, you may want to use visual aids as well as talking or ask your pupils to do something to help you communicate a particular learning point. It includes thinking about the lesson so that it involves a variety of activities, e.g. listening, watching, doing, as well as taking into consideration who the pupils will be working with (individual, pairs, groups). It is important to take all of these issues into consideration when planning and to ensure that pupils are clear about what you want them to learn, to do and to achieve.

Although differentiation is usually the teacher's responsibility, as a TA you may still need to differentiate when working with individual pupils or small groups, as well as needing to think about it if you are asked to cover whole classes during the teacher's planning, preparation and assessment time (PPA).

---

**Box 2.2 Disability equality and rights resources**

---

*Disability Equality in the Classroom – A Human Rights Issue*, is a handbook written by disabled educators Richard Rieser and Micheline Mason (1990). This book promotes equality in schools and it includes interesting activities and materials for both pupils and staff.

The Disability Rights Commission has also developed some lessons to address citizenship and disability for pupils in key stages 3 and 4. They include resources such as worksheets and videos and are freely available online at http://www.drc-gb.org/citizenship/

---

## Supporting for independence

One of the challenges facing TAs working with pupils with SEN is how much support to give and when. In a study *'Inclusion: what deaf pupils think'*, carried out by the University of Hertfordshire for the Royal National Institute for the Deaf (RNID), deaf pupils said how difficult it was to tell their support assistants to step back sometimes and let them get on with their work in their own time (Iantaffi et al, 2002). One of the pupils interviewed expressed the wish to be able to 'freeze' and 'unfreeze' the support according to need. This can be seen as a clear desire (especially by older pupils) to be in control of their own learning process, which includes being able to make their own mistakes. Nevertheless, if your job is to support a pupil's learning, it can be difficult to know when to intervene and how.

A concept that can be helpful in this context is that of 'scaffolding', developed mainly by influential psychologist Jerome Bruner. Scaffolding is based on the idea that, when we learn something new, we need as much support as we can get whereas, as our knowledge or skills develop, this support can be gradually withdrawn until it is no longer needed. This process happens several times during our lives and the degree of initial scaffolding required may vary, as can the length for which it is required. It does not just apply to curricular learning in school either; it can be applied to how we learn life skills. For example, the infant learning to feed requires his/her mother's full support initially but as he/she grow older, he/she becomes more and more independent until as a young adult, he/she can usually gather the food, prepare and eat it without any support. In a similar way, a pupil learning to read needs full support at first in recognising the letters, associating them with sounds and meanings, until he/she becomes an independent reader who no longer needs any support. As TAs you move along this continuum all the time and you need to make decisions on where to locate yourself.

Scaffolding implies that one of your aims, in supporting this pupil, is that they will become an independent learner, who no longer needs any support, or who needs only a minimum of support, according to his/her needs. This expectation is also modelled in our education system where in primary school you get much more support than in secondary school, for example, until you are expected to learn independently for great part of the time in further and higher education.

Knowing when to support and how much support to give can be tricky. You may need to be familiar with what it is reasonable to expect from a pupils at their particular age. For example, what can a 6-year-old be expected to achieve when learning about sequencing events in chronological order? Being familiar with age-related expectations is not enough as you also need to consider a pupil's level of maturity, needs and any external factors that might also have an impact on the learning process, such as the fact that it is the Friday afternoon before the summer break!

As well as considering these factors, it is also important to take a moment to think about your motivation for intervening while a pupil is carrying out a task. If they have made a mistake, would it be more useful for them to finish the task first and then be encouraged to revise what they have done? Are you worried about what the teacher might think? If the pupils you are working with have made several mistakes, do you worry that the teacher would take this as a reflection of your support? This may seem silly or inappropriate to some of you but, when training TAs, such worries (although hard to admit) can be present at times. After all, if you are employed to support a specific pupil or you usually support a particular group, it can be understandable that you may see their progress as a sign of your success as a TA.

Useful questions to ask yourself, if you recognise this pitfall, are:

■   *What is best for this pupil/group at this point in time?*

- *Should I intervene now, later or not at all?*
- *What is going to help them to learn best?*

If in doubt, ask the pupils themselves. You are a vital partner in their learning process so it is worth taking a little time to get to know your pupils' styles. Do they like getting on with their work and accept that they might make mistakes along the way? Or, do they prefer you to be involved in bringing things to their attention as they carry out their activities? Of course, the replies will vary according to the pupils' age, abilities and the teaching and learning activities in question.

Finally, when giving constructive support bear in mind that your task is not to do the work for them but to show them where the gap or mistake is and, if appropriate and necessary, giving guidance on how to fill or amend it (*Box 2.3*). In this way, you will be supporting not just your pupils' learning but their journey towards adulthood.

---

### Box 2.3 Seeing results

High quality teaching and support will only lead to high quality learning when children develop independent strategies through working harder.

Ask yourself who worked harder in the last session you had with a group of pupils – you or them?

If it was you, think back and see if you could have changed one strategy to make them work harder instead. Think about this next time you plan a session.

---

# Promoting behaviour for learning

Inclusive classrooms can also be challenging in terms of behaviour. To be a better TA you need to be confident in managing behaviour in the range of situations in which you work.

Whatever your background or experience there is always something new to learn or revisit regarding the principles of behaviour management. The key is to understand that you are only managing behaviour in order for all pupils to learn, not just to control them or even change their behaviour. Sometimes, just to remind yourself of this really helps in a challenging situation.

Behaviour is an emotional issue and you need to stand back and be able to disassociate challenging behaviour from the pupil and from yourself. Some pupils do find it hard to behave for a number of reasons – poor parenting, emotional disorders and low self-esteem. It is often difficult to believe that the most challenging behaviour – the kind that causes you to feel inadequate – comes from pupils with very low self-esteem.

In order to be confident in promoting behaviour for learning, you need to plan systematically to manage it.

Three simple rules for managing behaviour

- **be clear**
- **be positive**
- **be consistent.**

## Be clear

The first step is to be very clear about the school's behaviour policy (*Box 2.4*). Most school policies are based on the '4Rs' framework which outlines the:

- **Rights** – of pupils, staff and parents to learn, have respect and be safe.
- **Responsibilities** – of pupils, staff and parents to choose to behave in such a way so that everyone can enjoy their rights.
- **Rules** – describe the behaviours that will be seen. Do be kind and helpful. Do listen. Do look after property.
- **Routines** – recognisable daily patterns, e.g. moving round the school, answering questions.

Pupils are encouraged to make choices about their behaviour and understand the relationship between choice and consequence.

- A good choice will lead to a good consequence – a reward.
- A choice that infringes others' rights will have a negative consequence – a sanction.

### Be positive

The next step is to be positive when dealing with pupils.

- Positive language is very effective, both in impact on pupils and how it makes you feel, e.g. 'Stop calling out' becomes 'What is our rule for answering questions?' 'Get on with your work!' becomes 'What should you be doing now?' 'Then do it please!' Sometimes it is hard to be positive all the time but it is the most effective strategy you have. *Next time you are working with a group try to use only positive language and notice the effect.*
- Catch pupils being good rather than correcting them. This works with even the most challenging behaviour. Praising pupils for getting on with their work after time off task has more impact then a negative statement. As a general rule pupils should hear positive and negative remarks in a ratio of 6:1. *Try to listen to yourself and assess how well you are doing or ask someone to observe you and give you feedback.*

---

### Box 2.4 Behaviour policies

---

Behaviour policies enable all adults to work together consistently and positively across the school in order to promote a safe learning environment. Pupils are able to see fairness in the way they are managed by the staff, predict outcomes more easily and learn to accept responsibility for their own behaviour.

Class teachers sometimes have their own approach adapted from the school policy and often class rules, routines, rewards and sanctions are displayed in the classroom. You need to be aware of these. In some situations you will need to draw up your own rules, routines, rewards and sanctions for groups that you work with. Always ensure that all pupils are clear about their rights and responsibilities in relation to the rules and routines. Time invested in actively teaching and modelling good behaviour is always rewarded in a better climate for learning for all pupils.

There is now considerable evidence that developing children's social, emotional and behaviour skills is an important and effective way of improving children's behaviour, attendance and learning. By building these skills and by doing so progressively through the primary school years, lasting improvements can be made.

Is your school involved in a Behaviour Improvement Project (BIP) where the teaching of these skills is done throughout the school during assemblies and Personal, Health and Social Education lessons (PHSE)?

- Always remember to say please and thank you and include the pupil's name when making requests, this not only models good behaviour but has a positive impact on the pupil.

- Use the language of choice. This gives pupils the responsibility for their own behaviour and takes the stress out of confrontations leaving both you and them feeling confident and calm. For example: *'You are choosing not to do you work so you are choosing to...'* (whatever the school sanction is for that). All the responsibility is then on the pupil and often they will make the right choice and complete their work. Then you can catch them being good. *'Well done Sally for getting on with your writing'*

- Plan alternatives to confrontation and take control. Just as you plan for lessons to ensure that learning takes place so you need to plan to deal with any behaviour challenges. If you have thought through a range of possible strategies before hand you are in a much stronger position to successfully re-focus pupils on their learning.

## Be consistent

The final step is to be totally consistent in how you promote behaviour so that all pupils are able to learn.

- The school's policy must be well known and implemented consistently by all the adults in the school. When this does not happen problems can occur. You also need to be clear about when you need to get help with a challenging situation. *Is your policy implemented consistently by all the adults in your school? Do you know the member of staff who has overall responsibility for behaviour? Have you talked to them about issues that concern you?*

- Implement rewards and sanctions, as described in the school policy or classroom rules, on consistent basis. As long as pupils are clear about the expectations and the consequences you must not hesitate in giving a sanction for a wrong choice of behaviour. Once you have hesitated or given them a second chance, pupils will exploit your hesitation and it will undermine your positive behaviour management in the future. *Are you totally consistent in using both sanctions and rewards?*

■ Always try to focus on the primary behaviour, not the secondary. Sometimes this is very hard, but just ask yourself what was the original issue here? It is so easy to be pulled into arguments with pupils and end up not dealing with the original incident. *Can you think of a time that it has happened to you recently? How could you have managed the situation differently?*

■ Always build and maintain positive relationships with your pupils and ensure that you separate any inappropriate behaviour from the pupil. In keeping the focus on the behaviour, you are accepting that the pupil can get it wrong and make a mistake and it allows for changing to better behaviour.

Finally, don't struggle alone with behaviour challenges, if you are still having problems talk to someone! Your line manager, class teacher, SENCO...it is not a sign of weakness; it is a sign that as a professional you want to get it right for the pupils. All staff in a school, from newly qualified teachers to heads will struggle at sometime with behaviour management issues. Promoting behaviour for learning (*Box 2.5*) is the responsibility of everyone in the school and the more that adults work together and share their views the easier the job will become.

## Box 2.5 Useful resources for promoting behaviour for learning

As well as those in your school, there are numerous resources to support behaviour management; these are just a few that are easy to access and have been found to be useful by TAs.

- *Teaching Assistant File* – induction training for teaching assistants in primary/secondary schools (DfES, 2004d). This has a whole section devoted to strategies and approaches to positive behaviour management based on the 4Rs framework

- *Behaviour and Attendance: developing skills* (DfES, 2003d) – here you will find information on the Department's policies to promote inclusion and learning through positive behaviour. The site contains information on behaviour and bullying http://www.dfes.gov.uk/ibis/index.cfm

- *Primary National Strategy* (DfES, 2003a) – carried out a Behaviour and Attendance Pilot and these very useful materials are now available either in your school or on www.dfesstandards/gov.uk

- *Behaviour Management Effective Strategies* (BMEF) – this is a useful website with lots of practical ideas for dealing with all types of behaviour from incessant talking to answering back http://www.bmef.org/

- *Behaviour4Learning* – The focus of Behaviour4Learning is to develop skills and insights, which foster a classroom ethos of 'behaviour for learning'. This site is primarily for newly qualified teachers and is an excellent resource for TAs http://www.behaviour4learning.ac.uk/

## Handy Hints

- The inclusion agenda is driven by The Children Act 2004 and *the Special Education Code of Practice* (SEN COP) published by the government.

- An inclusive learning environment is one in which diversity is acknowledged and celebrated

- 'We are all different but we all have value.'

- Children have special educational needs if they have a learning difficulty, which calls for special educational provision to be made for them.

- The SEN COP recommends a graduated response to SEN, i.e. differentiation, school action, school action plus, request for statutory assessment and issue of a statement, if appropriate.

- Scaffolding learning is an important tool in supporting for independence.

- Promoting behaviour for learning in inclusive environments needs to be clear, positive and consistent.

CHAPTER 3

# IMPORTANT THINGS YOU NEED TO KNOW ABOUT SCHOOLS

Schools are complex organisations. Each one has its own particular character and identity with related challenges. In order to be a better TA, you need to understand something about the way schools work and your role in relation to that in your own school. You may be an experienced TA and know most of these things, in which case you could plan how you might use this knowledge to help other more inexperienced colleagues.

Whatever the setting or type of school you are working in certain things are common to all.

## HOW DO SCHOOLS WORK?

The head teacher is the key person in the school and works in partnership with the senior management team and the governing body to ensure that the school promotes the highest possible standards in all areas of the school curriculum.

The governing body has a wide range of responsibilities and powers. They:

- Help to raise standards of achievement.
- Plan the school's future direction.
- Appoint the head teacher and deputies.
- Make decisions on the school's budget and staffing.
- Implement a performance management policy for appraising staff.

- Make sure the national curriculum is taught.
- Set appropriate targets for pupil achievement at key stages 2, 3 and 4.
- Report test results to parents.
- Decide how the school can encourage pupils' spiritual, moral and cultural development.
- Make sure that the school provides for all its pupils including those with special needs.
- Are accountable for the performance of the school to parents and the wider community.
- Draw up an action plan following an Ofsted inspection.

This is a daunting list given that all governing bodies include parents, staff and governors and there is no salary! A number of TAs are governors themselves and this certainly helps them to have a very good understanding of the school and how it works.

## Statutory frameworks

All schools have to work within these:

- Children Act
- education law
- employment law.

### Children Act 2004

*Every Child Matters*, the Government's vision for all the agencies and organisations involved with children, was published in 2003 (DfES, 2003e). The green paper was printed in response to the death of Victoria Climbié, the young girl who was horrifically abused, tortured and eventually killed by her great aunt and the man with whom they lived. This case highlighted the urgent need for change in the way children's services worked together and were held accountable. The green paper prompted an unprecedented debate and wide reaching consultation with people working in children's services, and with parents, children and young people.

*Every Child Matters* is a new approach to the wellbeing of children and young people from birth to the age of 19 years. It explains how the new Children Act 2004 forms the basis of a long-term programme of change. This programme places better outcomes for children firmly at the centre of all policies and approaches involving children's services.

These outcomes are to:

- be healthy
- stay safe
- enjoy and achieve through learning
- make a positive contribution to society
- achieve economic wellbeing.

### Every Child Matters: Change for Children in Schools

This booklet describes the implication of the Children Act for schools and is one of a series produced for all the different services working with children*. It is a very important document, which outlines your role (whether you are a head teacher, a teacher, a TA, member of the support staff or a governor) in relationship to the new way of ensuring the highest standards for all children.

Schools and their governing bodies will consider the changes that are happening locally and particularly those regarding the planned development of extended services in and around schools.

---

\* Ask for a copy at school or download one from www.everychildmatters. gov.uk

Your school may already offer such services as breakfast and after school clubs. These have been shown to improve children's motivation and engagement. The Government is looking to all schools, over time, to provide a core offer of extended services.

- The outcomes in *Every Child Matters* are important to know – they form the basis of all changes to the way schools work and all new initiatives will need to take account of them.

## Education Law

The DfES is responsible for carrying out government education policy in England. *The National Curriculum* was revised and streamlined in 2000. The National Curriculum:

- Sets out the most important skills that every child has a right to learn.
- Is a legal framework given by the government to teachers so that all pupils are taught in a way that is balanced and manageable but hard enough to challenge them.
- Gives standards that measure how well children are doing in each subject – so that teachers can plan to help them do better.
- Enables pupils to have the same opportunities in their learning wherever they go to school.
- Provides a more inclusive framework than previous versions did.
- Requires teachers to have regard for setting appropriate challenges; provide for diverse needs; provide for pupils with SEN and support for pupils for whom English is an additional language.

The Foundation Stage happens before the National Curriculum and is a framework for learning from three to five years.

The Literacy and Numeracy strategies were introduced by the government to support teachers in raising standards (Each strategy was accompanied by a detailed framework and a large number of related training programmes for teachers and teaching assistants) (*Boxes 3.1 and 3.2*). For more detail see *Chapter 1*.

### Box 3.1 Stages, years, national tests and tasks

| Age | Stage | Year | Tests and assessments | Average expected levels |
|-----|-------|------|----------------------|-------------------------|
| 3-4 | Foundation | | | |
| 4-5 | | Reception | Foundation stage profile | |
| 5-6 | Key stage | Year 1 | | |
| 6-7 | 1 | Year 2 | Teacher assessment English and maths | Level 2+ |
| 7-8 | Key stage | Year 3 | | |
| 8-9 | 2 | Year 4 | | |
| 9-10 | | Year 5 | | |
| 10-11 | | Year 6 | National tests in English, maths & science | Level 4+ |
| 11-12 | Key stage | Year 7 | | |
| 12-13 | 3 | Year 8 | | |
| 13-14 | | Year 9 | National tests in English, maths & science | Level 5+ |
| 14-15 | Key stage | Year 10 | | |
| 15-16 | 4 | Year 11 | GCSEs or other national qualifications | |

### The wider curriculum

In addition to the subjects in the national curriculum, schools also teach religious education. There is no national programme for this and your school may follow the guidance of the Local Education Authority, the locally agreed syllabus or, if it is a church school, a programme related to that particular faith.

Other important areas for pupils to experience are PSHE, which help them to respect and value the richness and diversity of our society. Your school's brochure will explain how each subject is taught at your school and the brochure is a good starting point for you to understand your school's curriculum and the emphasis that is placed on different subjects or areas.

---

### Box 3.2 The Learning Journey

The best way to get a quick overview of the National Curriculum, the different subjects covered and the list of things that pupils are taught and expected to know by ages five, seven, 11, 14 and 16 years old, is to obtain copies of :

*The Learning Journey* - choose from Foundation and Key Stage 1; Key stage 2; Key stage 3; Key stage 4

Call DfES order line 0800 0966626 or download a copy from www.parentcentre.gov.uk

*Flyers containing the key points are available in a number of languages, which are very useful if you are working with families whose first language is not English.*

---

## Planning for learning

How do teachers manage to teach the whole curriculum?

The Qualifications and Curriculum Authority (QCA) and commercial companies have produced detailed schemes of work to help teachers plan for and teach all the subjects of the curriculum. Schools first produce long-term plans to show how they will cover all aspects of all the subjects during a pupils' time at school. To make it easier to cover everything (especially in key stages 1 and 2) and make it much more enjoyable for the pupils, subjects are often combined into topics, e.g. food, water, journeys, Victorians. This plan is often called a curriculum map. Then, for each term or half term there will be medium-term plans to show in more detail what will be taught for each year group.

Teachers then use these to plan for their class on a daily or weekly basis. They identify what they want their pupils to learn, how they are going to teach and most importantly, how they are going to assess the pupils' progress. These short-term plans are adapted to the individual needs of their class. The weekly or daily plan is often where you as a TA come into direct contact with the planning and the best plans show you what the children are expected to learn in each session, teaching methods, grouping, resources and what your role will be.

Giving feedback to the teacher on how the pupils perform is the key factor that will support the teacher in planning the next step in the pupils' learning.

Teachers have more flexibility in how they produce their plans since the introduction of the *Primary National Strategy* (DfES, 2003a) and the publication of *Excellence and Enjoyment* (DfES, 2003b). They just need to be clear about what they want the pupils to learn, how that fits into the big picture of medium- and long-term plans and how it will enable them to make progress.

To support the teaching of individual subjects, schools normally appoint a teacher who has special responsibility for overseeing the subject. These teachers draw up a policy to show how the subject will be taught and assessed, order and manage the resources to support learning and most importantly, act as an adviser to other staff – including TAs. So, for example, if you have questions regarding a science topic you are involved with, the science coordinator could be a very useful resource for you (*Box 3.3*).

---

### Box 3.3 Curriculum resources

---

- One of the best resources to support you with subjects in the curriculum that are unfamiliar to you, can be found on www. parents.dfee.gov.uk/discover.

- Leaflets relating to the QCA schemes of work identify what children will be learning at school in different subjects. For example, a year 1 leaflet about plants records what pupils will be learning in school and also gives practical and detailed ideas for work at home. These leaflets provide very useful background reading for you if you wish to be more prepared for class topics or for planning cover lessons.

- Equally good is the website National Curriculum in Action (http://www.ncaction.org.uk/). This website uses pupils' work and case study materials to show what the National Curriculum looks like in practice. The examples for each subject show the standard of pupils' work at different ages and key stages, how the programmes of study translate into real activities and effective use of ICT across the curriculum.

- Check out www.curriculumonline.gov.uk. On this website you'll find all the multimedia resources to support teaching and learning that your school can buy with its e-Learning Credits (eLCs), which are substantial funds (provided by the government) for your school to spend on multimedia resources in the form of eLCs. All resources support the curriculum taught in schools in England from Foundation to KS4. Many are free (http://www.curriculumonline.gov.uk/help/curriculumonlineisfree.htm). Evaluate and compare resources before buying direct from suppliers.

## How are schools monitored?

Local Authorities have a duty to monitor and challenge schools so that they provide the best possible outcomes for all their pupils. Each year governing bodies and head teachers set targets for their pupils in key stages 2, 3 and 4. Results from the national tests and examinations in key stage 2, 3, 4 and A levels are published annually*. Schools are judged against the results and the progress each individual pupil has made.

### The school profile

Following the passage of the Education Act 2005, governing bodies are no longer required to hold an annual parents meeting nor to produce a governors' annual report. The School Profile has replaced the report. The format of the profile has been agreed following extensive consultation and includes data on the school's performance supplied by the DfES.

* You can search for all schools' results on this site http://news.bbc.co.uk/1/hi/education/4624596.stm

The School Profile will also include the following headings:

- What have been our successes this year?
- What are we trying to improve?
- How have our results changed over time?
- How are we making sure that very child gets teaching to match individual needs?
- How do we make sure that our pupils are healthy safe and well-supported?
- What have we done in response to our last Ofsted report?
- How are we working with parents and the local community?

This profile will provide an invaluable resource for you as a TA and answer lots of questions about important things you need to know about the school. More information can be found on www.governornet.co.uk (follow the link from the home page). Profiles will also be live from spring term 2006 on www.parentcentre.org.uk.

## Ofsted

The Office for Standards in Education (Ofsted) was set up in 1992 to evaluate the work of schools and publish the findings so that parents had information about the quality of education provided for their children. As with everything connected with schools there have been numerous changes to the inspections and the latest inspection framework was introduced in September 2005 to take into account the Children Act 2004 and *Every Child Matters* (DfES, 2003d).

Previously, schools had been given lengthy notice regarding a forthcoming inspection and this put a great deal of unnecessary pressure on staff and actually worked against improving standards as time was taken to 'prepare' for the inspection. Under the new framework schools have only two to three days notice, the actual inspection only lasts up to three days and the report is produced within three weeks. The new approach is putting much more responsibility on schools to objectively evaluate and 'inspect' their own performance. All schools are completing a self-evaluation form (SEF), which is then used by the inspectors as the basis for the inspection. Exemplar SEFs are available on the Ofsted website (www.ofsted.gov.uk).

The areas for evaluation are:

- characteristics of the school
- views of learners, parents and carers and other stakeholders
- achievement and standards
- personal development and well being
- the quality of provision, including the quality of teaching
- leadership and management
- overall effectiveness and efficiency.

Schools have to look at all these areas and grade themselves for each section and then give themselves an overall grade. Next, they identify areas they need to develop further to improve or maintain their grade and ensure the best outcomes for pupils.

The school improvement plan is the key document that outlines the key priorities that the school is working on each year to continue to raise standard and to respond to new initiatives.

You may have been asked to make contributions to your school's SEF and it is a good idea for you to have a copy, if possible, as it enables you to understand the strengths of your school and areas to develop as identified by the head teacher and senior management team.

The report following an inspection is now only four pages long and gives the inspection team's judgement on the effectiveness of the school which can be outstanding, good, satisfactory or requiring improvement. A letter is also sent to the pupils telling them the good things about the school and the areas the inspectors have identified as needing improvement.

- Have you seen a copy of your school's most recent Ofsted report? If not, you can find it on the Ofsted website www. ofsted.gov.uk
- Do you have a copy of the current school improvement plan?

## Employment law and key policies

The work of schools is governed by a number of policies and statutory frameworks, which are important for you to know about. You cannot be expected to read and memorise all the information but rather you need to be clear about the important documents and polices and know where to find them if you need to look things up. Of course, you may have been given your own copy of these policies when you first started working at your school. If so, make sure you still have the most up-to-date versions, as schools should regularly review their policies to reflect both governmental and societal changes.

Some schools publish handbooks for staff with all the key policies and information, if your school is not one of these use your mentor or class teacher to help you locate the following polices and guidelines.

### Health and safety

Employers are required to have a health and safety policy and to ensure that their employees understand it. All schools must observe their employer's health and safety policy and

any directions given by them by their employer in respect of health to this area. The head teacher will, in practice, be responsible for enforcing the health and safety policy day-to-day*. Schools may also add to this policy to take account of their own particular circumstances to ensure the health and safety of pupils while in school, e.g. in laboratories, studios and workshops, in physical education, during break times and on educational visits.

You need to be aware of the health and safety policy so that you can organise and ensure that you manage safely the learning activities, physical teaching space, and any resources for which you have been given responsibility.

---

* See more details about all areas covered at
  http://www.teachernet.gov.uk/management/atoz/h/healthandsafety/
  and http://www.hse.gov.uk/

## Behaviour

The behaviour policy is one of the most important in the school. It lays down clear expectations for behaviour, outlines the rights and responsibilities of the pupils, staff and parents and finally, sets out a list of sanctions and rewards. It is recommended that schools revisit this policy annually as it has such a vital role in ensuring consistency across the school and enabling children access to learning. See *Chapter 2* for more information about behaviour policies.

## Equal opportunities

The Race Relations Amendment Act 2001 places a legal obligation on all staff in a school to promote racial understanding and harmony. Sometimes TAs think that it does not apply to their 'mainly white school' but racial incidents can occur at any time and it is important that you know the school's definition of a racial incident and the correct procedures to follow for reporting. Sometimes the race equality policy is incorporated in the equal opportunities policy. Ask for help if you are unable to find it. Nearly all TAs we have worked with instinctively challenge all forms of inequality from calling pink a girls' colour to ensuring both girls and boys are able to play for the netball team. However, it is still important to find the policy and guidelines and ensure that you always follow them and challenge any stereotyped views or harassment*.

## Child protection

All schools come under the Children Act and have a child protection policy and guidelines. All staff should know the identity of the designated person to whom child protection issues are to be referred. As a TA you are often in a position to notice

---

* Test your knowledge of anti-discrimination issues online at http://www. stop-discrimination.info/ – an EU campaign for diversity.

signs of abuse and you should be vigilant for these signs, which are not always physical. Child protection training is now part of the DfES induction course for newly appointed TAs and it is vital that you undergo regular training.

If a pupil does reveal anything to you ensure that you follow the school guidelines and do not do anything to jeopardise the process. Listen carefully and as soon as possible write down what was said and date it. Never ask questions or give opinions. It is not your place to decide if the pupil is telling the truth – that will be the responsibility of the designated person.

Associated with this there should be school guidance on intimate situations and you need to be aware of these and follow them carefully. Some schools ask TAs to work in pairs when cleaning up toilet accidents. Schools should be a place of safety for pupils but as TAs you must take account of your own vulnerability and ensure that for instance, you never comfort upset pupils in private places. Men are particularly vulnerable here and should not put themselves in a position that may lead to misunderstanding.

There may be pupils in your school who some times require restraint this is another area where you need to be very clear about the guidelines and be properly trained in the correct procedures.

More information about issues of child protection in school can be found on Teachernet (http://www.teachernet.gov.uk/childprotection).

## Workforce remodelling

For the last 22 years schools have been subjected to a number of radical reforms and changes, all introduced to ensure that pupils get the best chance possible of achieving high standards of education. These changes have put extra burdens on staff and increased the amount of paperwork to be completed. The recent introduction of PPA time and workforce remodelling has been designed to alleviate this and free teachers to concentrate on their core business, that of progressing the learning of pupils. One of the principles in the national agreement was recognition of the contribution support staff makes in raising standards.

Ofsted recently published a report into the impact of the workforce reform called *Remodelling the School Workforce* (2005).

The key findings were:

- Following the reduction of bureaucracy and the delegation of clerical/administrative tasks, teachers have benefited from increased support in the classroom and are able to focus to a greater extent on improving the quality of teaching and learning.
- Most schools have integrated support staff within school management structures. In the majority of schools visited there were high levels of job satisfaction among support staff.
- In many of the primary and special schools, the TAs who would usually be working with the whole class are providing supervised cover.

If you are a HLTA or often asked to cover classes, you need to be aware of the school's policy relating to cover for PPA time and know your rights. The official website dealing with remodelling in school, including national agreement and extended schools programmes can be found at http://www.remodelling.org/

## What next for schools?

There will continue to be radical changes in schools over the next decade. All these changes will be driven by the principles of

*Every Child Matters* (DfES, 2003d) and for the first time take into account the 'whole child'.

Learners only flourish if education successfully adapts to the needs and demands of the time. This year some 600000 eager children will start school. They will leave their mark on the 21st century. The quality of the school and curriculum they meet is crucial to their development. To meet this challenge, the National Curriculum is due to be revised and both the literacy (DfES 1998a) and numeracy (DfES, 1999b) frameworks are currently undergoing revision.

In October 2005, the DfES published the Schools White Paper: *Higher Standards, Better Schools for All – More Choice for Parents and Pupils*. This White Paper sets out plans to radically improve the system putting parents and the needs of their children at the heart of our schools, freeing up schools to innovate and succeed and bringing in new dynamism and new providers. It will ensure that every school delivers an excellent education, that every child achieves to their potential and that the system is increasingly driven by parents and choice. To make that happen we need an education system that is designed around the needs of the individual with education tailored to the needs of each child and parents having a say in how schools are run. To achieve that we need to reform schools themselves so that they have the freedoms and flexibilities to deliver the tailored, choice driven education we all want*.

---

\* Read more in *A New Relationship With Schools: the Next Steps* (DfES and Ofsted, 2005)
http://publications.teachernet.gov.uk/eOrderingDownload/1288-2005DOC-EN.pdf

### Handy Hints

- School governing bodies have a wide range of powers and duties.

- *Every Child Matters: Change for children in schools* (DfES, 2003d) explains the implications of the Children Act 2004.

- Curriculum 2000 (http://www.curriculum2000.co.uk/) is a legal framework setting out what schools must teach and age related expectations for pupils.

- School profiles have replaced the governing body annual report and are available on line.

- Ofsted have a new inspection framework based on school self-evaluation.

- Teaching assistants need to be familiar with four key school policies.

- Schools and education law is continually changing in an effort to raise standards children and young people.

CHAPTER 4

# WORKING WITH OTHER ADULTS

One of the biggest challenges that many TAs face is working with other adults. A team of hard-working TAs underpins the best schools and the happiest TAs are the ones who are valued by their colleagues as a crucial part of the team. Schools vary tremendously in how they deploy the different adults that are part of the team and that includes the TAs; you will find the differences in how schools work with TAs between can be startling. Often the support staff in the school have been there the longest, are members of the local community and know the children and families better than anyone else on the team. If this is recognised as a fundamental asset to the team as a whole then everyone will benefit.

## Teaching staff

Recently the lines have begun to blur between the teaching and support staff; a big part of a HLTAs role is often to teach, so do they count as support staff or teaching staff? This is an issue that is being addressed currently and causes a lot of debate between teachers and TAs alike. Again, it is one where schools vary enormously and one that will only develop further as more and more TAs gain the status of HLTA. Watch this space!

However, despite the debate, every class is still required to have a qualified teacher assigned to them and these are what we will talk about here as the teaching staff.

The DfES (2000b) guide to *Working with Teaching Assistants* states that '...*both teacher and TA need to be aware of their different functions.*

*The teacher plans lessons and directs learning. The TA provides support to the teacher and through this to the pupils and to the teaching of the curriculum. The TA works under the direction of the teacher, whether in the whole class or on their own with a small group of pupils or an individual...'*. In the case of HLTAs this role is extended considerably and will be looked at in later chapters.

It is generally accepted that the happiest TAs are those that have the chance to develop mutually supportive working relationships with the class teachers that they are assigned to. In some cases this will be the class teacher of the class that they work with every day, in others this will be the variety of teachers they work with as they move around the school supporting particular children. Either way it is vital that they are given the chance to develop their relationships and the time to communicate about short- and long-term issues.

A good partnership is what is needed and it needs to have certain features:

- shared aims and objectives
- shared understanding of how to reach those objectives
- clearly defined roles for each partner
- clearly defined and mutually agreed allocation of work
- sufficient time allocated to reaching shared goals
- a sense of humour on both sides
- an understanding of what to do when things go wrong.

Of course, in an ideal world this would be the norm in every classroom but in the real world, other things will get in the way, not least the children. As long as both partners have some understanding of this then most problems should be resolved without too much difficulty.

One of the areas that can cause problems is the issue of roles. If you ask most young children about the adults that work in their classes they will have some understanding of who does what, although not necessarily what their job titles are. Often they will say that the TA is their 'helper' or that the TA is the one who sorts out their reading diaries etc. Issues can arise as the children get older and they will pick up on tensions between adults if they exist. It is for these reasons that class teachers and TAs working with older children (and some of the younger ones!) need to be very clear as to the status given to the TA and how to challenge the inevitable 'you're not a proper teacher!' comment (*Box 4.1*).

---

### Box 4.1 Communication tips

---

Some of the everyday language that we use can communicate volumes to the children and will go a long way to showing them that you and the class teacher are a team.

- Refer to each other when you are reminding the children about behaviour or expectations.
  *'I'm sure Mrs Carter wouldn't expect to see you doing that!'*

- Make it clear that you both have the same expectations.
  *'How do Mr Walker and I expect you to sit on the carpet?'*

- Be positive and share your praise of the children
  *'Jamie tried really hard today so we will give him a sticker.'*

- Back each other up.
  *'I hope you're working really well for Mrs Carter like you did for me yesterday.'*

The children need to know that the adults are working as a team and that they will back each other up, as will senior staff in the school and (hopefully) the parents. This kind of teamwork is especially difficult when TAs work in a wide range of different classes, and because of this, needs to be worked on even harder. The same principles apply but need to be repeated according to different situations and settings. *Working with Teaching Assistants* (DfES, 2000b) states that '...some teachers are not used to sharing their classrooms with other adults. They may restrict TAs to performing routine tasks, hence allowing them to provide only a low grade of support to the teacher...'. This is becoming less and less common, but still occurs in some classrooms. It is something that can be addressed through specific job descriptions for the TA that are accepted and understood by both parties and, as such, is a management issue for the school.

Inevitably, problems will arise but the school should have systems in place to address these and if not, maybe you will be able to learn from your situation to benefit you in the future! When you are lucky enough to have a mutually supportive relationship with the class teacher it can make a world of difference to you and the children so, it is something the whole school should be involved in working for.

## Leadership team

Senior management or leadership teams have a direct influence upon how successfully TAs work within their schools. They need to ensure a wide range of whole school factors including:

- differentiating and defining the roles of class teacher and TA
- reviewing progress and setting professional development goals as a part of performance management

- ensuring TA involvement in planning
- encouraging high quality TA input
- developing feedback mechanisms
- establishing behaviour management procedures that recognise the TAs role
- including TAs in staff training and INSET
- ensuring TAs are informed of children's needs and background as appropriate
- including TAs in SEN reviews as appropriate
- including TAs in written communications
- informing TAs of their legal responsibilities, e.g. health and safety and child protection.

The main aspect that can cause contention is the definition of roles and responsibilities between the class teacher and TA and it is essential that the TA has a clear and precise job description that all parties are happy with. These roles need to be redefined regularly (*Box 4.2*) as TAs develop professionally and they need to be offered opportunities to extend their knowledge and skills according to both their own and the school's needs. The most successful schools seem to have TAs working in varied, defined roles that are clearly structured by the management team. These TAs are offered appropriate professional development as they need it and are encouraged to share their expertise with other members of the team. They attend staff meetings, planning meetings, all forms of INSET and are involved in SEN review meetings for the children that they work with. Of course, this doesn't happen in all schools and is very much dependent upon the attitudes of the leadership team within the school. Some schools show aspects of this; others still won't let TAs into the staff room! The variety is quite startling. If you find yourself in a school where the leadership team do not recognise the role that TAs play you may need to bear this in mind – things are moving forward, but more slowly in some places than others!

---

**Box 4.2 Resources on the net**

---

- www.teachernet.gov.uk has advice for TAs and management staff on various aspects of the role and how it relates to other adults
- www.tda.gov.uk also has advice for both TAs and HLTAs.

## Support staff

Support staff roles can vary enormously from TA to admin, caretaker to ICT technician; they all have a vital part to play.

Recently the roles of support staff have diversified further as a response to the workload agreement. There are now schools that employ support staff to take on duties that were formerly considered to be part of the teachers' role. This includes HLTAs who routinely take responsibility for areas of the curriculum, such as music and for teaching classes during PPA time and cover lessons.

Within this team of support staff it is vital that the roles are clearly defined and laid out and that the team works well together as a whole. One of the most productive ways to support each other as a team of TAs is by having regular meetings where issues can be raised and addressed. In many schools this will be led by a senior member of the teaching staff, for example teams of TAs who support in SEN will have weekly meetings with the SENCO. This way issues that arise with the children can be addressed as a team. It improves communication between the TAs, keeps the SENCO informed of the children's progress and provides a valuable support network for all involved. In others, there will

be a senior TA who will take on the role of coordinating the sessions, or maybe the deputy or head will be involved – it varies greatly from school to school.

Without such meetings issues may arise that cannot be addressed and lack of communication could lead to serious weaknesses in the team as a whole. Often, time is set aside as part of the working week for these meetings. The school will feel the benefits and as such, they should be given the priority they deserve. If you are working in a school where this doesn't happen it is worth suggesting; even if you just meet quickly during assembly time, it's a start!

In some areas schools have taken a step further and have introduced cluster meetings where the TAs from several schools in the same area get together to receive training and discuss issues in the community. This can also be enormously beneficial and is maybe something for us to look to in the future. Many schools will also have meetings between all the support staff to address common issues, for example, the office staff may need to communicate something to the midday assistants and TAs about a child's home circumstances, the caretaker (or site care manager) may need to tell about issues to do with the site itself...the list goes on. These don't need to be as regular as the TA meetings but there is definitely a place for them.

# External specialists

Many TAs will get the chance to work with a variety of different external specialists within their role, especially those that work with children with SEN. If you support a child one-to-one for much of the week you will find that you will become the person who knows them best and therefore, the person who should attend review meetings to assess their progress and plan future targets. Depending on the nature and degree of the child's difficulties, you may come across a variety of professionals whose expertise you can learn from. This is just a small sample of the ones you are most likely to come across:

## Specialist Support Teachers

These are usually very experienced teachers with particular specialisms, e.g. dyslexia, who may work one-to-one with the child or who may support you by giving you activities and resources to use in the classroom.

## Behaviour Support Workers

These tend to be teachers or experienced TAs who will work with the child (sometimes the family) to manage their behaviour. They may be able to give you training in behaviour management techniques and ideas for resources.

## Educational Psychologists

These are often experienced teachers who have gone on to train as educational psychologists (EPs). They will be able to assess the child's strengths and difficulties and suggest targets and strategies to help meet those targets. In some areas you will come across assistant EPs who are experienced teachers who have had some training but have yet to go on and train as an EP.

## Speech and Language Therapists

Children with specific speech and language problems will need the support of a speech and language therapist. They will be able to assess the child's difficulties and give you activities and resources to use in school.

## Occupational Therapists

Occupational therapist's role tends to be in enabling children with specific mental or physical disabilities to gain more independence. They will help with assessment of the child's abilities and will be able to give you specific activities or exercises to support the child at school.

You will find that the help and advice you get from some of these specialists will be invaluable, so take the opportunity to work with them whenever possible. Some senior TAs will take on the responsibility for writing IEPs from these review meetings – again an example of the TA's expanding role.

# Parents

A lot of TAs who work with older children will have no face-to-face contact with parents at all; others will be their main point of contact. The main differences here are in the attitudes of the school. Despite the fact that any contact you have with parents is minimal, it is still vitally important for the child and parent as well as the school.

Often when children start school the class teacher and TA for the foundation stage will make a home visit or will invite parents into school to introduce themselves. This is the first step in making the parents feel part of their child's education and will set the pattern for the coming years. Many parents find TAs more approachable than the class teacher, especially if they are anxious and don't want top appear to be 'pestering' the teacher, so you may find that you are able to 'bridge the gap' and develop some good relationships. You may also find that you are the person that parent-helpers will come to for guidance and advice. These are important parts of the TA role.

Other contact may come in your contribution to home-school diaries – maybe for reading, behaviour or general progress. This contact is vitally important to most parents in the early years when their children are at school and your notes or comments can have a lot of impact.

Comments in reading diaries need to be positive and constructive, e.g. *'Well read Rosie'*, doesn't tell a parent anything. It might be useful to have a bank of comments to address particular areas, e.g. *'Well read Jack, next time remember to take a breath at full stops'*, *'Danny tried really hard to use voices for the different characters'* or *'Liam was able to tell me what had happened so far'*.

Often, TAs are part of a school's local community and as such, have a particular insight into the children's backgrounds that teachers may not have access to. In this case, it is important to recognise the need for confidentiality – you may hear things in the staff room that should not be communicated to parents but conversely you may be able to give the teachers invaluable background information about families that will enable them to teach the children better. Here, there is a need to follow policies and procedures and it is best to find out what these are in individual schools.

## Governors

Contact with governors may be limited but it is important to appreciate their role. Often, a member of the support staff will be on the governing body and as your representative they should communicate the main points to you. More information about the role of school governors can be found at www.governornet.co.uk or directly from your school.

### Handy Hints

- Schools are all different but they all rely on teamwork.
- Teaching assistants are vital to the success of the school.
- Happy teaching assistants are those who know what their role is and how to carry it out successfully.
- Communication among teaching assistants and within the school as a whole is key.
- Teaching assistants should to be aware of what the roles of other adults are within the school.
- Work with parents and external agencies are important parts of the teaching assistant's role.

CHAPTER 5

# LOOKING AFTER YOURSELF

Schools can be stressful environments. Using your break to gather materials for the next lessons or speak to a colleague may have become habits. You may even cover an additional role within your school during lunch breaks, such as midday or dining hall supervision. Time is a precious commodity, which is usually dedicated to others rather than yourself. The most common complaint shared by TAs during training courses on any topic, from behaviour to planning, is usually 'but there just isn't enough time to do this!'

This chapter will not magically increase the amount of time at your disposal but it will encourage you to think about your priorities and how you spend your time. After all, you are the most precious commodity for yourself, your family and your school!

## Knowing your duties and your rights

The role of the TA has changed enormously over the past decade. Initiatives such as the HLTA status and the increased profile of TAs in schools indicate that this is now a profession in its own right with a developing career path. Yet, in our experience, many TAs do not see themselves as professionals and can often be unaware of both their rights and their responsibilities (*Box 5.1*).

It is easy to dismiss job descriptions and appraisals as paperwork or something that 'just does not apply' to you. However, if you want to look after yourself, it is vital to know whether you do indeed have a job description and what its contents are. For example, are you employed to work with named pupils and/or to assist teachers in their duties? Are you expected to clean up bodily fluids or to run after-school clubs? Most TAs' job descriptions will involve a range of duties. Knowing what these duties are mean that you can be effective at your job by focusing your time and effort on your actual duties rather than just responding to colleagues' requests. If your job description is very different from your everyday activities, it may be time to review your contract with a member of the senior management team, such as the head teacher or their deputy (depending on your school).

Appraisals can be the ideal time to discuss something like this. Seeing these opportunities as 'management checking up on you' can be a common myth. A well-planned and carried out appraisal should be the ideal forum for both employer and employee to review how the working relationship is going. It could be your chance to ask for further training or a pay rise to match increased (or new) responsibilities. Nevertheless, such conversations can be difficult to have, especially if you have not had an appraisal before or are not aware of your rights. In this case, unions can be a useful resource. The best appraisals include an observation of your work and provide feedback for you on your strengths and possible areas for you to develop in order to become a better TA. Observations often cause anxiety but once they are over it can be very pleasant to hear good things about your work with pupils and very useful for you to have areas identified for you to improve. If you have never had a formal observation of your work talk to your line manager, class teacher, senior TA or other appropriate person and find out if they can arrange one for you.

Being a member of a trade union is not just for those TAs who may be having difficulties within their schools. Unions represent their members in national negotiation over changes in role and pay. They often offer additional benefits such as free advice or members' discounts and special offers. Should you run into any difficulties with your school, it can be really helpful to feel supported by a union through its representatives.

As well as considering becoming a member of a union (if you are not one already) you also need to be aware of relevant documents and initiatives in order to better know your rights. One of such documents is the *Working with Teaching Assistants: A Good Practice Guide*, published by the DfES (2000b). Although this guide was written for teachers, heads and deputies, it can give TAs a better insight into their role within schools. Being familiar with the issues related to the national remodelling in schools is also important as those have an impact on your role. For example, the introduction of guaranteed PPA time has meant that several TAs in schools (mainly primary), especially if they are HLTA candidates, are being asked to teach whole classes under the teacher's supervision. Since teachers are not meant to plan lessons to be covered during PPA time, TAs often need to widen the range of skills at their disposal in order to fulfill their responsibilities effectively.

---

### Box 5.1 Checklist

---

- Do you have a job description? If so, do you have a copy or know where you can find it? When was it last reviewed? Are you aware of its contents?
- Do your day-to-day activities reflect the contents of your job description?
- Do you know who your line manager is? Do you have regular appraisals?
- If your role within the school has changed, has your contract been renegotiated?
- Are you a member of a union? Do you know if your school has a union representative for teaching assistants?

# Feeling part of a professional team

You may feel comfortable with your duties most of the time but it is likely that, at some point in your professional career, you will meet a more challenging task or responsibility. For many of you, this may have already happened if you have embarked on the HLTA training and, as a consequence, you may have taught a whole class for the first time. Alternatively, you could have met a child whose behaviour you have found difficult to handle. No matter what the scenario, any professional will sometimes feel as if they do not have enough knowledge, skills or experience. Schools are particularly challenging environments in this regard as you are continuously asked to deal with both adults and children across a range of developmental stages and often with a whole range of subjects (unless you are a secondary TA dedicated to a particular department). Many TAs enjoy the fact that no day (or even hour) may be the same in school; yet, this is also the biggest challenge of any educator.

The good news is that no professional is doing their job alone within a school. You are part of a community, which includes children and parents and a professional team. This is an invaluable resource when you know how to tap into it. You can probably think of at least one example of when working successfully in partnership with a colleague has enhanced your practice and made you a better TA. Nevertheless, working collaboratively with others does involve some conscious efforts by all parties. For example, you need to be aware of your strengths and limitations so that you can both offer and ask for help when necessary and appropriate. You also need to feel safe and confident enough to be able to ask for support from your colleagues. The school culture plays an important part in creative a collaborative atmosphere but it is also true that every person working in the school contributes to its culture. It is a circular process of which you are part.

If you are not sure about who to go to for advice what can you do to find out? It may be a platitude but being able to ask for advice and support is strength for any effective teaching professional. Nobody can be expected to know everything all the time.

You can also learn to be assertive. If something is getting in the way of you carrying out your duties or interfering with your well being you do need to take action. The majority of TAs who we have worked with feel it is not appropriate for them take up teachers' time to discuss such issues as they feel that teachers are already 'too busy and have to much to do'.

However, it is worth you leaning to be assertive, which really means being very polite but firm and asking to talk to your line manager or, if appropriate, the head teacher (*Box 5.2*). It always pays to ask for something that is important to your role as a TA and to make your feelings known. As long as you do it pleasantly you have nothing to lose and everything to gain!

---

### Box 5.2 Case study

Two TAs on the assessment-only route preparing to be assessed as HLTAs, were very stressed about the amount of work that they had to complete in such a short time. Their tutor suggested that they asked to talk to their head teacher about the situation. The TAs were very sceptical but did as suggested. The outcome was very positive and gave them two paid half-days each to complete their portfolios and an apology from the head for not noticing their difficulties!

# An effective and happy TA

One of the reasons you may be reading this book is likely to be about wanting to improve your practice and hopefully, being happy within your role. This chapter has pointed out some key areas that you may want to look at more closely, yet ultimately, looking after yourself is something very personal. You are the only one who can truly look at your professional life and identify what is already working for you or where there may be room for improvement.

In the opening of this chapter, we stated how you might feel that there is not enough time to do anything other than what you do already. If this applies to you, we would encourage you to take just half an hour to look at your day in school. How is your time spent? Try and account for every minute of your workday. Are there any tasks, such as tidying resources, that could be carried out by someone else (maybe the pupils themselves)? Remember that part of learning for the pupils in your care is to be as independent and responsible as it is appropriate to their age and abilities. Are you spending your time carrying out duties laid out in your job description or are other things taking up part of your day? If your skills and experience would be better used doing something else, it could be time to talk to your classroom or head teacher.

Finally, as stated earlier, you are an asset, not just for yourself and your family but also your school. Take a moment to reflect on what you need the most in order to better look after yourself. It may be that you need to accept the fact that you are indeed a professional with clear and wide-ranging duties as well as rights. Alternatively, you may need to re-evaluate how you spend your time and choose what needs prioritising. Regardless of what your specific professional needs may be, don't forget to look after your health, both physical and mental. Schools are demanding environments and you may spend the rest of your time looking after others in your personal life too. It can be easy to forget

how vital taking some time out for yourself is. However you may spend such personal time, we invite you to take this time as part of looking after yourself.

---

### Box 5.3 Resources on the net

- **The National Association of Professional Teaching Assistants**
  (http://www.napta.org.uk/)
- **The Professional Association of Teachers (PAT)**
  An independent union for professionals allied to teaching, including TAs. http://www.pat.org.uk/
- **UNISON**
  Britain's biggest trade union for people delivering public services. (http://www.unison.org.uk/)

- **Learning Support**
  A high quality, full-colour magazine for teaching assistants, learning support assistants, learning mentors, nursery nurses, mealtime and playground supervisors and every other member of the primary school team working with children. Every issue of Learning Support is packed with lively but expert features about the children you work with and their needs, practical ideas and tips and all the news affecting school support staff. It is published twice a term (six times a year). More details at www.learningsupport.co.uk

- **TA awards**
  Look at this site to see colleagues who have been nominated for awards – you could be next! http://www.teachingawards.com/

## Handy Hints

- Teaching assistants are professional members of the school team.
- Teaching assistants need job descriptions which accurately reflect their duties.
- Teaching assistants are strongly advised to join a union.
- Teaching assistants should take care of themselves both professionally and personally.

**CHAPTER 6**

# TAKING STOCK: THE WAY FORWARD

There is no requirement for TAs to have any qualifications or training before taking up a post but as the role of the TA is changing so drastically, there are now far more opportunities for professional development and a wide range of different training routes that will help you progress.

## Self review

Before you consider your training needs it is useful to examine what parts of your current role are beneficial and which parts you would like to change – try answering the following questions:

- What aspects of your current role do you find the most satisfying?
- What parts give you the least satisfaction?
- What aspects of your current role would you like to do more of?
- Do you have skills that you think could be better used? How?
- Are there any new tasks that you feel you would be able to take responsibility for?
- Are there any tasks or areas that you would like to receive further training in?

Once you have answered these questions and given some thought to the areas that you would like to progress in, you need to talk to your school leadership team to find out what their opinions are. Communication is vital here as they may already have a training route that they would like you to follow or, they may feel that you don't need any further training and should remain in your role as you are. If your job description states that you work 25 hours, one-to-one with a statemented child then it's very unlikely that you will be given the chance to become the school ICT technician without a lot of negotiation! Often, your long-term aims may take several years of 'small steps' progress in order to reach your ultimate goal. Lots of TAs have a teaching qualification as their ultimate aim; others just want to find out more about their current role, with huge variation in between.

# Training

If you decide that you want to take steps in getting further training you need to find out whether it can be done through the school, e.g. on local authority training days or whether you need to look outside the school at colleges and providers in your locality.

There is a bewildering array of courses available for TAs from level 1 key skills, level 2 (equivalent to GCSEs grades A–C), level 3 (equivalent to A level) through to foundation degrees. There is more explanation of these in the document 'Guidance on Qualifications for Teaching Assistants' which can be accessed from www.lg-employers.gov.uk or via www.teachernet.gov.uk as below.

There are two main kinds of general qualification at levels 2 and 3 that TAs can access (*Box 6.1*):

- Vocationally Related Qualifications (VRQs) – these are linked to national occupational standards and are more suited to those who prefer a more study-based training programme. They include some work-based assessment as well as assignments, projects and sometimes, short written tests.

■   Qualifications (National Vocational Qualifications; NVQs)
    – these are firmly based on national occupational standards
    and look closely at the candidate's competence to do the
    job to the standards required.

---

### Box 6.1 Some examples of courses available

**Vocationally-related qualifications**    **Occupational qualifications**

**CACHE** Level 2 Certificate for Teaching Assistants
**NCFE** Level 2 Certificate for Teaching Assistants
**Edexcel** Level 2 BTEC Certificate for Teaching Assistants
**ABC** Level 2 Certificate for Teaching Assistants
**OCR** Level 2 Certificate for Teaching Assistants (submitted for accreditation)

**NVQ** level 2 for Teaching Assistants (awarded by CACHE, OCR, City & Guilds and Edexcel)

**CACHE** Level 3 Certificate for Teaching Assistants
**Edexcel** Level 3 BTEC Certificate for Teaching Assistants
**NCFE** Level 3 Certificate for Teaching Assistants
**OCR** Level 3 Certificate for Teaching Assistants (submitted for accreditation)

**NVQ** level 3 for Teaching Assistants (awarded by CACHE, OCR, City & Guilds and Edexcel)

**NCFE** Level 3 Certificate for Teaching Assistants
**OCR** Level 3 Certificate for Teaching Assistants (submitted for accreditation)

More information on the providers listed can be found from the related websites listed in Box 6.2.

As well as the courses given above, there is also the option at level 2 and 3 of Modern Apprenticeships. These are not a qualification as such, rather a package of qualifications designed originally for young people up to the age of 25 years.

The other option that is available at level 3, and in some cases at level 4, is the wide range of locally developed Specialist Teaching Assistant courses. These are locally developed and delivered training programmes that are aimed at TAs who have been in post for at least one year. Due to the fact that they are locally delivered, they do vary in level and whether they count towards entry onto degree level training. Some universities offer higher education qualifications, such as certificates or diplomas of higher education, specifically for TAs. These are often developed and delivered in partnership with Local Education Authorities. However, Certificates and Diplomas of Higher Education for TAs are increasingly being incorporated into relevant foundation degree programmes.

There is now a wide range of foundation degrees for teaching assistants from different providers. They have a variety of titles such as Foundation Degree Teaching & Learning Support and Foundation Degree in Educational Studies for Teaching Assistants. Most focus on either primary or secondary (both covering those working in special schools), however, some providers offer both primary and secondary courses in parallel. As foundation degrees are developed and delivered by groups of higher and further education institutions, there will be local access to a relevant foundation degree in most parts of the country. They offer progression opportunities to a related honours degree, which for teaching assistants wishing to teach in primary schools could provide a route to Qualified Teacher Status (QTS).

# Higher level teaching assistant (HLTA) status

This is the latest big initiative in TA professional development and is currently one of the biggest areas of both debate and contention in schools up and down the country.

Unlike the other training described above, this is not a qualification but a status. It is recognition that an individual is operating competently against a set of national standards defined by the Teacher Development Agency (TDA). These standards are arranged in areas covering professional values and practice, knowledge and understanding and teaching and learning activities. They include the expectation that the candidate is able to teach whole classes, advance the children's learning and has done so on more than one occasion. Other courses and training that TAs have undertaken will help them to reach these standards and show that they are working at this level. They will not, however, count towards the assessment.

There are now two preparation routes to access HLTA status. The first is assessment-only where candidates are supported in collecting evidence to show that they are meeting the standards but are not trained in any aspect of their role in school. It is expected that candidates accessing this route will have evidence of level 2 qualifications in English and Maths, and will have the support of the head teacher that they are already working at the level expected within the standards. They will receive three days preparation (out of school) on how to complete the tasks and evidence all the standards. The second route will take a modular form according to the identified training needs of the candidate against the standards, and will be followed by the three-day route described above. This will be followed by a school assessment visit where an assessor will make a judgment of the candidate's competence on the basis of their collected evidence and through interviews with the relevant teaching staff, the head teacher (or representative) and the candidate. This judgment will then be moderated by the provider and communicated to the TDA and candidate. More information on the process, standards and providers can be found at www.tda.gov.uk/support

---

### Box 6.2 Resources on the net

Some of the best websites to research what courses are available to you:

- http://www.standards.dfes.gov.uk
  This site gives details of the TA induction course, which is aimed at new TAs working in YR to Y6 and focuses mainly on the literacy and numeracy hours, along with behaviour management.

- http://www.teachernet.gov.uk/wholeschool/
  teachingassistants/
  In this site you will find information about teaching assistants in general, it also has very useful links to the *Guidance on Qualifications for Teaching Assistants,* which is useful to LEA providers, school managers and TAs alike.

- http://www.learndirect-advice.co.uk
  This gives you an overview of the different levels of training available and who the main providers are.

- http://www.open.ac.uk
  You can find information here about a whole range of Open University courses, including ones specifically focussed on teaching assistants. This is a good place to find out about distance learning if you want to work towards a degree.

- http://www.tda.gov.uk/support
  This is the main site for accessing information about Higher Level Teaching Assistant Status (HLTA).

---

The following websites will give information on specific courses:

- www.ncfe.org.uk
- www.edexcel.org.uk
- www.cache.org.uk
- www.city-and-guilds.co.uk

Finally, if you have managed to finish reading this book, you will have hopefully realised that you already are a very good, caring and professional TA!

# BIBLIOGRAPHY

## REFERENCES

Alpin R (1988) *Assisting Numeracy: A handbook for teaching assistants.* BEAM Education, London

Commission for Racial Equality (2001) *The Race Relations Amendment Act 2000.* CRE, London

DfES (1998a) *National Literacy Strategy.* DfES Publications Centre, Annesley, Nottingham

DfES (1998b) *Literacy Hour.* DfES Publications Centre, Annesley, Nottingham

DfES (1998c) *The National Curriculum.* DfES Publications Centre, Annesley, Nottingham

DfES (1999a) *The Spelling Bank.* DfES Publications Centre, Annesley, Nottingham

DfES (1999b) *National Numeracy Strategy.* DfES Publications Centre, Annesley, Nottingham

DfES (1999c) *NNS Teaching written calculations - guidance for teachers at key stages 1 and 2.* DfES Publications Centre, Annesley, Nottingham

DfES (2000a) *Mathematical Vocabulary.* DfES Publications Centre, Annesley, Nottingham

DfES (2000b) *Working with Teaching Assistants* – A Good Practice Guide, DfES Publications Centre, Annesley, Nottingham

DfES (2001) *Early Writing and Grammar for Writing.* DfES Publications Centre, Annesley, Nottingham

DfES (2002a) *Special Educational Needs Code of Practice*. DfES Publications Centre, Annesley, Nottingham

DfES (2002b) *The DfES Code of Practice*. DfES Publications Centre, Annesley, Nottingham

DfES (2003a) *The Primary National Strategy*. DfES Publications Centre, Annesley, Nottingham

DfES (2003b) *Excellence and Enjoyment – A Strategy for Primary schools*. DfES Publications Centre, Annesley, Nottingham

DfES (2003c) *NLS Professional Development resource pack 1*. DfES Publications Centre, Annesley, Nottingham

DfES (2003d) *Behaviour and Attendance: developing skills*. DfES Publications Centre, Annesley, Nottingham

DfES (2003e) *Every Child Matters*. Green Paper. DfES Publications Centre, Annesley, Nottingham

DfES (2004a) *ICT Across the Curriculum*. DfES Publications Centre, Annesley, Nottingham

DfES (2004b) *Five Year Strategy for Children and Learners*. DfES Publications Centre, Annesley, Nottingham

DfES (2004c) *NNS Teaching Mental Calculation Strategies - guidance for teachers at key stages 1 and 2*. DfES Publications Centre, Annesley, Nottingham

DfES (2004d) *Teaching assistant file: Induction training for teaching assistants in primary schools*. DfES Publications Centre, Annesley, Nottingham

DfES (2005) *Higher Standards, Better Schools for All - More Choice for Parents and Pupils*. White Paper. DfES Publications Centre, Annesley, Nottingham

Fox G, Halliwell M (2000) *Supporting Literacy and Numeracy: A guide for learning support assistants*. David Fulton Publishers, London

Gardner H (1983) *Frames of Mind: the Theory of Multiple Intelligences.* Basic Books, NY

Haddon M (2003) *The Curious Incident of the Dog in the Night-time.* Vintage, London

House of Commons (1996) *The Education Act 1996.* HMSO, London

Hughes M (1986) *Children and Number: Difficulties in Learning.* Blackwell Publishing, Oxford

Hull J (2004) Teaching as a Trans-World Activity. *Support for Learning* **10**(3)

Iantaffi A, Sinka I, Jarvis J (2002) *Inclusion: what deaf pupils think.* Royal National Institute of the Deaf (RNID) Publications, London

Kline N (1999) *Time to Think: Listening to Ignite the Human Mind.* Cassell Illustrated, London

Ofsted (2005) *Remodelling the School Workforce.* Ofsted Publications Centre, London

Rieser R and and Mason M (1990) *Disability Equality in the Classroom – A Human Rights Issue.* Inner London Education Authority, London

# FURTHER READING

Bruner J (1960) *The Process of Education,* Harvard University Press, Cambridge, Mass

DfES & Ofsted (2005) *A new relationship with schools: the next steps.* DfES Publications Centre, Annesley, Nottingham

Kline N (1999) *Time to Think: Listening to Ignite the Human Mind.* Cassell Illustrated, London

# USEFUL WEBSITES

**All accessed April 2006**

**www.basic-skills.org.uk** Website for the Basic Skills Agency.

**www.becta.org.uk** British Educational Communications and Technology Agency.

**www.blueskiesproject.org.uk** A website dedicated to the use of ICT with deaf children and young people.

**www.cache.org.uk** Information of courses.

**www.city-and-guilds.co.uk** Information on courses.

**www.curriculumonline.gov.uk** The National Curriculum online.

**www.edexcel.org.uk** Information on courses.

**www.governornet.co.uk** The site for school governors.

**www.learndirect-advice.co.uk** This gives you an overview of the different levels of training available and who the main providers are.

**www.learningsupport.co.uk** A high quality, full colour magazine for teaching assistants, learning support assistants, learning mentors, nursery nurses, mealtime and playground supervisors and every other member of the primary school team working with children.

**www.mathsnet.net** Useful site for maths resources.

**www.napta.org.uk** The National Association of Professional Teaching Assistants. This is a network offering membership

**www.ncaction.org.uk** This will give you detail and explanation about all areas of *The National Curriculum* and show examples of pupils' work.

**www.ncfe.org.uk** Information on courses.

**www.open.ac.uk** You can find information here about a whole range of Open University courses, including ones specifically focussed on teaching assistants. This is a good place to find out about distance learning if you want to work.

**www.parentcentre.gov.uk** Excellent information site for parents.

**www.pat.org.uk** An independent union for professionals allied to teaching, including TAs.

www.remodelling.org The official website dealing with remodelling in school, including national agreement and extended schools programmes.

Read more:

**www.school-resources.co.uk** An educational resource website offering interactive information technology quizzes, and a library of learning and teaching resources to staff and students.

**www.standards.dfes.gov.uk** The Department for Standards in Education. This site gives details of the TA induction course which is aimed at new TAs working in YR to Y6 and focuses mainly on the literacy and numeracy hours, along with behaviour management.

**www.stop-discrimination.info** EU campaign for diversity including an opportunity to test your knowledge of anti-discrimination issues online

**www.tda.gov.uk/support** Site of the Training and Development Agency. This is the main site for accessing information about Higher Level teaching Assistant Status.

**www.teachingawards.com** Look at this site to see colleagues who have been nominated for awards – you could be next!

**www.teachernet.gov.uk** In this site you will find information about teaching assistants in general, it also has very useful links to the Guidance on Qualifications for Teaching Assistants which is useful to LEA providers, school managers and TAs alike.

**www.timetothink.com** The site for Nancy Kline, author of Time to Think: Listening to Ignite the Human Mind.

**www.unison.org.uk** Britain's biggest trade union for people delivering public services.